PLAYSONGS

Action songs and rhymes for babies and toddlers

Compiled by **Sheena Roberts**
Performed by **Sandra Kerr** *and* **Leon Rosselson**
Illustrated by **Stephanie Ryder**

PLAYSONGS PUBLICATIONS LIMITED

Please check for CD at back.

Contents

All the songs are performed on the cassette / CD and the track numbers are given below in brackets.

For Charlie, Jacob and Rachel
and all the other babies who helped
to choose these songs and rhymes

Introduction

This is a collection of songs and rhymes to help you make singing and exploring sound an everyday part of your baby's life.

Playing singing and rhyming games with our babies and toddlers gives them the best possible start they can have in music-making. And, best of all, no music specialist can do a better job than us, our children's special adults.

This is because babies and toddlers experience music most intensely through the physical and emotional contact they have with the people who care for them most closely. We wouldn't dream of sending our babies to a linguist to teach them to talk – think how much they would miss! The same goes for music. Don't delay your child's musical life until she is 'old enough to start piano lessons'. Just as she learns to speak, feed herself, draw, dance and cuddle through imitation of you, so she will learn to sing and love music-making.

The combination of sound and physical contact at this age is fundamental. Singing alone is good, for the sound of your voice is in itself a close bond between you; but singing as you rock your child in your arms, bounce her, dance with her, tickle her, dress her, bath her and play with her on your knee is the most valuable and direct musical experience you can give.

Why is there a need for this book, if music-making is so natural a part of young children's lives? A lot of us, including myself when my first child was born, are out of practice in singing and have lost touch with the repertoire of playsongs which is part of folk tradition. And, while your baby will be happy with whatever you sing to her – whether rock song or grand opera – it is those songs that involve physical play that are especially valuable.

Age range

Most of the songs included here can be sung from birth right through to the end of toddlerhood; it is what you do with them that changes. For example, the song I habitually used to calm my crying, colicky five-day-old baby was *One two three* (page 15). I held her firmly against my shoulder, her head supported by my hand, and danced, or rather jogged up and down as I sang. This had an almost one hundred per-cent success rate. As she got older, I started to play some of the actions with her – patting her tummy on 'one two three', touching her eyes, stretching her arms up then down – before dancing round with her. By about the age of one she was beginning to imitate the actions herself, and by age two she could do it completely unsupported, and was beginning to sing it herself.

You know best what your baby or toddler is ready for, but don't be afraid to try sooner rather than later – even if it is just *you* doing the actions, *she* will be taking it all in. But in general, rocking, dancing (with her in your arms), touching, tickling and peekaboo come first, followed by the playsongs you can do when she can sit up firmly (about six months). These are the leg-walkers, bouncers and pony-trotters. Then come the fingerplays and action songs, in which she will be starting to do the actions herself (do them for her before she reaches this stage). Soundmakers span the whole age-range, as do washing songs, dressing and going out songs, and, of course, lullabies.

Overcoming your inhibitions

If you yourself don't enjoy songs and games like these, you may not think that this is the right book for you. But before you put it down, ask yourself *why* you don't think it is for you. Perhaps you feel inhibited about singing out loud, or dancing around, even if the only one in the audience is the baby. If this is so, perhaps you *do* need this book – and just a little bit of courage to get started. If you are one of those people who was always asked to mime when singing at school and consider yourself to be tone-deaf, bear in mind that your voice is still the most important sound in your child's world. She will not mind what your singing voice is like; to her it is magic. Just take a deep breath, relax your vocal chords, and sing!

When to sing and play

Certainly not as a dutiful daily exercise! As far as the baby is concerned, any time can be the right time to sing the songs. When she is grizzly and unhappy, a lullaby may soothe her, or a bouncy dance or tickling song can change her mood instantly to smiles and chuckles. Nappy-changes are often good times for touching and tickling songs. When she is warm, relaxed and happy after a feed and a sleep, it might be a good time for an action song, fingerplay or for introducing a sound game as you play together. If you find that things are getting on top of you (your child is taking ages to walk the last hundred yards to the front door, or struggling so much you can't get her pullover on), an appropriate song may not only save the child from screaming, but you as well. Singing is a great way to release tensions. I often found when singing my second baby to sleep, that the lullaby was as much for my benefit as for his.

Using the cassette/CD

This is lovely to listen to, thanks to Sandra and Leon, but *your* voice is still more important to your child. Use the recording to learn the songs, but don't use it to replace you.

Use the words printed in the book as starting points rather than something to be learned by rote. Change them to suit your own needs. Your child, once she is old enough, may improvise freely of her own accord, but you will give her even more confidence to do so, if you try it yourself. (Likewise, if you forget the melody, make it up.)

Starting a baby music group

By the time my first baby was one, I had gathered so many songs that I thought I would like to share them with other people whose repertoire was, as mine had been, rusty or non-existent. Gathering weekly in a small carpeted room in our local community centre, we spent about 45 minutes sitting on the floor in a ring, singing and playing with our children on our knees. They ranged from newly-born babies to toddlers, and the group soon expanded to three sessions. The babies loved these sessions, and gained something extra from being with other babies and adults – music is, after all, a social as well as an individual pleasure. We found they were remarkably attentive, and particularly quick to imitate as they saw not only their own adult clapping, touching their ears or wiggling their fingers, but others as well – and all at the same time!

You do not need a community centre to set up a baby music group. Your own living room floor will do equally well, and an informal coffee meeting can be a good opportunity. However, it is important to put toys out of sight until afterwards, and to concentrate on the singing for the whole session – as soon as you start chatting to each other, the babies will, not surprisingly, crawl off to amuse themselves.

It helps to have someone leading the singing. This only involves being prepared to start first, a little louder than the others, and deciding which verse to sing next. But don't expect one person to lead all the time; everyone can take a turn. Don't be afraid to repeat a rhyme or song many times. Babies adore repetition. Choose a speed to suit the children – they tend to need plenty of time to grasp changes in actions and words.

What you can expect to achieve

The aim of all this is not to produce musical whizz kids, though if you do have musical ambitions for your baby, this is a good way to start. Playsongs *will* help your child to sing, and to gain a good sense of rhythm, and sharpen her interest in sounds. But the most important thing to be gained is sheer enjoyment for both you and your child. Playsongs precede toys in the order of games that you and your baby can play together, and they are among the most intimate pleasures you can share. If you gain from them a child who sings confidently, improvises freely, and explores sounds with fascination, look on it as a bonus, but never forget the enjoyment of the process for its own sake.

Sheena Roberts.

Can you play at peekaboo?

1

Can you play at peekaboo?

2

I can play at peekaboo,

3

Are you there?

4

Yes I am! (repeat)

5

6

Peeka-peeka-peeka-peeka-BOO!

◄Peekaboo is one of the earliest games your baby will enjoy, and it will remain a firm favourite right up until you have a child who is ready to play hide-and-seek.

In the song, hide your face behind your hands and peek out at the end of each line. On the final big 'BOO!', throw both your hands away from your face. Repeat lines three and four if you like, and you can draw out 'peeka-peeka' to add to the surprise of the last boo.

Babies and small toddlers: lightly cover ► her face with a headsquare as you sing, then whip it off quickly at 'BOO!' Repeat. (For babies who don't like to be covered you can hold up the material as a screen between you.)

Try hiding a soft toy behind your back and jumping it out at 'BOO!':
Where oh where is Nina's little teddy,
Where has the teddy gone? – BOO!
(Repeat)

Or use the song like *Jack-in-the-box*, sitting the baby between your knees and jumping her high in the air on 'boo'. You might also hide a bell or rattle and shake it instead of saying 'boo':
Where oh where is Julia's rattle
Where has the rattle gone? – (shake)
(Repeat)

Bigger toddlers: sing it as you play hide-and-seek, but don't say 'boo' until you find each other.

Where oh where?

Where oh where is
  our little Nina,
Where has our
  Nina gone? – BOO!

Where oh where is
  our little Nina,
Where has our
  Nina gone? – BOO!

Jack-in-the-box

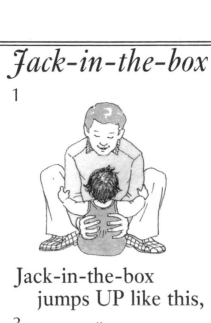

1

Jack-in-the-box
jumps UP like this,

2

He makes me laugh
  when he waggles
  his head,

3

Gently I press him
down again,

4

But Jack-in-the-box
jumps UP instead.

▲
Babies and small toddlers: make a 'box'
for her to sit in between your knees. Start
singing very quietly, then on 'UP', jump
her loudly out of her box and hold her
high in the air. Waggle her, then lower her
back into the box, ready to spring out
again in the last line.

Bigger toddlers: some will want to do all
the actions themselves and may like to
hide inside a large cardboard box. At line
three, put a firm hand on Jack's head to
press him down into his box.

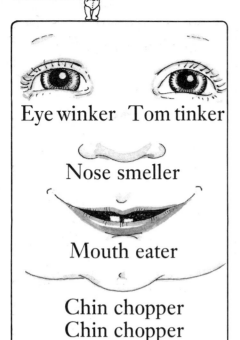

Eye winker   Tom tinker

Nose smeller

Mouth eater

Chin chopper
Chin chopper
Chin

▲
Gently touch each of the baby's eyes, then nose and mouth. On 'chin chopper', chuck her under the chin on each word. Add on the following lines for toddlers, who can touch each part themselves:

   Chin chopper
   Broad shoulder
   Arm waver
   Bread holder
   Chair sitter
   Knee knobbler
   Shoe stamper
   Tippy toe, tippy toe, tip.
(Tickle toes, or stand on tiptoe)

Clap clap clap

Clap clap clap your hands,
Clap your hands together,
Clap clap clap your hands,
Clap your hands together.
(Clap her hands in yours)

Round and round and round your tum,
Round and round we go,
Round and round and round your tum,
(Stroke her tummy in circles)

Then run up to your thumb.
(and tickle it)

▲
Babies and small toddlers: cradle her on your knee, or, if she is relaxed, play it while you prepare her for a bath or change a nappy.

Change the words of the first part to:
   Tap tap tap your feet . . .
   Shake shake shake your hands . . .
   Touch touch touch your nose . . .

And change the last part to:
   Then run up to your nose/mouth/hair/
   down to your toes/knee etc.

Bigger toddlers: they can do all the actions of the first part themselves and many more – stamping feet, jumping, tapping their shoulders. In the second part, dance round together and flop down at the end:
   Round and round and round we go,
   Round and round and round,
   Round and round and round we go,
   Then drop down to the ground.

Spots spots spots

Spots spots spots spots,
Spots spots spots spots,
A leopard has lots
of spots,
What a lot of spots
he's got.

A tiger has stripes
like long thin pipes,
But a leopard has lots
of spots,
Spots spots spots spots

Knock at the door,
(Tap her forehead
on each word)

Pull the bell,
(Tug a lock of hair)

Lift the latch,
(Tweek her nose)

And walk in.
(Walk your fingers
on her lips)

▲

Babies and toddlers: cradle a small baby in one arm while with your free hand you gently poke at imaginary spots all over her. In the tiger part, stroke your finger in long stripes over her body. Bigger toddlers can do this themselves.

Change the leopard words to include your child's name and the patterns or colours she is wearing:
Flowers flowers flowers flowers . . .
Katy's all covered in flowers . . .

Change the tiger words to:
A pussycat's fur
Is as warm as her purr
(Stroke her hair)

An elephant's nose
Is as long as a hose
(Tap her nose. Toddlers can wave one arm like a trunk)

You can add more actions for toddlers to do for themselves:
Shut the door
(Close one arm across chest)
Wipe your feet
Shake hands
And take a seat.

9

Little Peter Rabbit

1  **2**

Little Peter Rabbit's got a fly upon his nose,
Little Peter Rabbit's got a fly upon his nose,
Little Peter Rabbit's got a fly upon his nose,

3  **4**

So he swished it
and he swashed it,

And the fly flew
away.

5  **6**

Powder puff ——
Powder puff ——
Powder puff ——

He swished it and
he swashed it

and curly whiskers,
and curly whiskers,
and curly whiskers,

And the fly flew
away.

Tommy
Tommy

Tommy
Tommy Whoops

Tommy Whoops
Tommy

Tommy Tommy
Tommy

▲
Bigger babies and toddlers: touch the point of each finger in turn, starting with the littlest, as you say 'Tommy' – or the child's name. On 'Whoops', slide your finger down from her index fingertip to her thumb tip. Immediately reverse the order.

Small babies: in turn, touch her chin, lips, nose and forehead as you say 'Tommy' or her own name. On 'Whoops', slide your fingertip from her forehead to the tip of her nose, finishing with two 'Tommies' on her lips and chin.

◄ **Babies and small toddlers:** keep the actions very simple. Tap her nose (1–2), swish an imaginary fly away and buzz it up into the air with your fingers (3–4), then pat her bottom (5).

Bigger toddlers: give her a lead and let her do the actions herself. Don't be afraid to slow the song down to accommodate her speed, and don't worry if all she wants to do is tap her nose or wiggle her ears all through!

Sounds to touch

Sound wall

This is fun to make, and new things can be added or swopped for old ones to renew the baby's interest. Collect materials which make interesting sounds when they are touched — crinkly paper, plastic egg boxes, tinfoil dishes, corrugated paper, sandpaper, velcro, zips, strings of pasta, bells, milk-bottle tops, buttons, shells, etc. Firmly sew, staple and glue your collection onto a backing sheet of strong material and attach it to a wall.

A frame like a clothes horse can also be used and has the advantage of allowing things like saucepan lids to swing freely and make better sounds, but it must be carefully secured so that it cannot topple on the child.

Keep a variety of beaters handy so that the baby can experiment with tapping or scraping as well as touching – you could offer a metal, wooden or plastic spoon, egg whisk, pastry brush, large paint brush, strip of cardboard or ruler.

Activity sound centre

Attach items like a bicycle bell, hooter, bunch of keys, sucker, and piece of corrugated paper to a wooden board.

Sound box

Keep together a collection of sound-makers — shakers, saucepan lid and wooden spoon, biscuit tin, bells, rhythm sticks, yoghurt pots, etc. – to bring out as needed.

Ticklebird

1

2

Ticklebird, ticklebird —— fly round your nose,
Ticklebird, ticklebird —— fly round your nose,
Ticklebird, ticklebird —— fly round your nose,

3

And then you take
a peck!

4

Tickle here, tickle there,
tickle everywhere,
Tickle here, tickle there,
tickle everywhere.

▲
Your fingers fly round the baby or toddler in circles, ready to dart in and peck a nose, then tickle her all over. Change nose to ear, finger, toes, etc. Or change ticklebird to ticklemouse, running your fingers all over her body, then into

hiding in a sleeve, pocket, shoe, up her jumper, or behind her back:
Ticklemouse, ticklemouse
run round the house . . .
Then run away and hide!
Tickle here, tickle there . . .

Wee wiggie
Poke piggie
John gristle
Tom thistle
And old gobble
gobble GOBBLE

▲
Point to or stroke each finger in turn, starting with the littlest, then pretend to gobble up her thumb.

A little frog
lived in a hole,
Softly softly softly,
When all was quiet
as quiet could be,
OUT
popped
he!

Teddybear teddybear

1

Teddybear, teddybear,
touch the ground,

2

Teddybear, teddybear,
turn around,

3

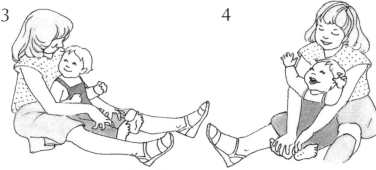

Teddybear, teddybear,
walk down the street,

4

Teddybear, teddybear,
tickle your feet.

There was a
little mouse,

Who sat in a chair,

When the cat said –

MIAOW

He ran right up
the stair!

▲
Bigger babies and toddlers: sit on the floor together as you help her with the actions. Big toddlers will be able to do the actions on their own, or can have fun helping their own teddybears to do them. Keep the actions going throughout, changing them on 'turn', 'walk', and 'tickle'.

Change the words of parts 3 and 4 to:
Walk up your clothes . . .
. . . tickle your nose.
Climb up the stair . . .
. . . tickle your hair.
Small babies: before she has learned to sit up you can sing this version for her as she

lies on her back or in your arms:
Teddybear teddybear,
touch your tum,
(Pat her tummy)
Teddybear teddybear,
here's your thumb. (Kiss it)
(And so on with 3 and 4)

13

Rock rock rock my boat

Rock rock rock my boat
 gently on the stream,
Merrily merrily
 merrily merrily,
Life is but a dream.

Row row row my boat gently down the stream
Merrily merrily merrily merrily, life is
 but a dream.

◄ **Small babies:** as she lies on her back and grips your fingers, rock her from side to side. If she is old enough, pull her up to sitting with these words:
Pull pull pull my boat
 up the hill to me,
Down down down again
 to float upon the sea.

Bigger babies and toddlers: make a boat for her between your outstretched legs, hold hands and row to the words of the second verse. Change to:
. . . quickly down the stream
. . . slowly down the stream

What shall we do with a lazy Katie?

Heave   ho

What shall we do with a lazy Katie? What shall we do with a lazy Katie? What shall we do with a lazy Katie? Early in the morning.	Roll her on the bed and tickle her all over, Roll her on the bed and tickle her all over, Roll her on the bed and tickle her all over, Early in the morning.	and UP she rises, Heave ho and UP she rises, Heave ho and UP she rises, Early in the morning.

You can dance with your baby in your ▶ arms from her birth onwards, and the rhythm and movement will soothe her when she is tired or colicky, and give her huge enjoyment when she is in a bouncy, playful mood.

Choose music to suit her need from your own singing, or from recordings of folk, pop, or classical music – whatever you enjoy.

By'm bye (page 44) is a lovely song to croon to her as you rock her when she needs soothing, and the song on this page is ideal for a bouncy dance.

Small babies: dance with her in your arms as you sing the song.

Bigger babies and small toddlers: hold her under the arms and do the actions of the first verse for her. Jump her up and down on 'one two three', touch her eyes with your fingertips, swing her into the air on 'sing it high', and down to the ground on 'sing it low'. Hold her arms out to her sides on 'for everyone', and wrap your arms and hers round her in a big cuddle on 'and me'. In the chorus, hold her under her arms again and jump her round in a circle. Alternatively, just dance with her in your arms if she doesn't want to do the actions.

Bigger toddlers: as she gets bigger you will be able to add more verses and actions. By about the age of two she may be ready to play it as a ring game holding hands with other children (particularly if they are older).

One two three

One two three, open your eyes and see

Sing it high and sing it low for everyone and me.

The left must take the right all around the ring,
We've got to keep the circle moving, everybody sing –

(Repeat the first verse for babies)

One two three,
open your eyes and see,
The sun has made the
    flowers grow

(Stretch arms up in a wide arc,
crouch down then rise up on tiptoe)

for everyone and me.

Out of the earth the
    root

(Crouch and slowly grow)

Out of the root the tree

(Stretch up high)

The tree bears the fruit

(Hands into fists)

The wind sets it free.

(Sway from side to side)

(Repeat from beginning)

Tārangam – dance away my little one

Tārangam tārangam
Veṇu Krishna tārangam
(Repeat

Dance away my little one,
  Dance little beauty,
Dance magic flute player
    Dance away on ocean waves.
    Dance away on ocean waves,
    Dance away on ocean waves.

Butter crazy little Krishna,
  Do you want to eat butter?
Butter cookie I will give you,
    Dance this way, dance that way.
    Dance this way, dance that way,
    Dance this way, dance that way.

Ocean waves, ocean waves,
  Rock this way, rock that way.
Pearls in the ocean waves,
  I see smiles in your face.
    Rock this way, rock that way,
    Rock this way, rock that way . . .

Dancing toys

You can make dancing toys, which jingle and rustle as they move, out of any available scrap – yoghurt pots, buttons, cotton reels, milk bottle tops, macaroni. Use materials which will make nice sounds when they dance.

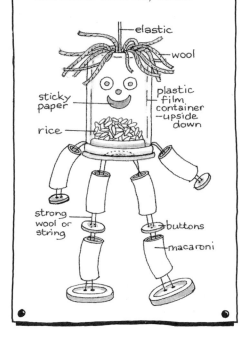

elastic
wool
sticky paper
plastic film container –upside down
rice
strong wool or string
buttons
macaroni

◀ An Indian dance song specially for a baby who is just taking her first unsteady steps. Sing it as you encourage her to walk towards you. Steady her with your hands, and when she lets go, click your fingers or clap in time to her steps. The changing rhythm of the repeated last line is sung for fun – it reflects her wavering, hesitant footsteps.

Macaroni girl

This is macaroni girl,
She would like to
    dance and twirl,
La la la la la la la
La la la la la la la
Curtsey low then
    off you go.

▲ Dance your homemade toy to this little song, changing the name as appropriate. Or, dance a soft toy instead:
Here is our friend dancing Ted
He can dance upon his head! . . .

Stop-go dancing

Pre-record some dance music on to a cassette, and insert gaps of about four seconds' silence in the music by pressing down the record button every so often as you play it through. You are now ready to play stop-go dancing.

Dance with your baby or toddler while the music is playing, and stop when it stops. During the silence, you can stand very still, you can tumble down to the floor, pull a silly face, wave your arms, or run quickly to a sofa and flop down onto it.

Everybody says sit down

Everybody says
    sit down, sit down,
Everybody says
    sit down, sit down,
But I can't sit down,
No, I can't sit down,
'Cause my feet are all
    full of dance around.

Jump up, jump up,
    dance around,
Everybody, everybody
    dance with me,
Jump up, jump up,
    dance around,
Everybody, everybody,
    dance with me.

▲
Babies: sit her on your lap and jog her as you sing the first verse, then jump her up in the air and dance her feet on your knees during the second.

Toddlers: sit down with her on the floor, wagging a finger at each other during the first verse, then both jump up and dance in the second. Change 'dance around' to an action like toe touching, stretching up high, jumping around, side bending or running on the spot – a great way for you both to get some exercise on a rainy day:

Jump up, jump up, touch your toes,
Everybody, everybody, bend down low . . .

The first verse (change 'sit down' to 'lie down' if you like) will give you a chance to recover and think of the exercise for the next verse!

Ring a ring o' roses is a lovely sit down and jump up dance for babies who are just walking. You can play it with her even before she has had courage to let go of your hands and walk alone.

I can hear Daniel walking down the street

I can hear Daniel walking down the street,
Tap tap tap tap, listen to his feet.

Leg over leg
as the dog
went to Dover,
When he came
to a stile,

(Cross and uncross her legs)
JUMP he went over.

Ankle bells and contrast sounds

For all these leg walking songs and rhymes it is fun to use ankle bells and rattles. Sew about ten little bells onto two bands of ribbon or elastic, which can then be slipped over the baby's ankles.

Wooden beads or macaroni can replace bells on one anklet to give a contrasting sound.

Bigger toddlers can dance wearing the anklets.

◀ **Babies and small toddlers:** you can do this simple little foot tapping song with your child on your knee while you walk her feet in the air, or tap them lightly on the edge of a table. (Very small babies can lie on their backs while you waggle their feet). Keep the rhythm very steady.

Change the pace to running, hopping (tap one leg), jumping (legs together), skipping, stamping, dancing, and so on.

Change it to the sounds her feet might make going through puddles, leaves, mud:
*I can hear Sandra splashing
    in the rain,
Splish splosh, splish splosh,
    all awash.*

Bigger toddlers: they can walk, stamp, jump, or tiptoe on their own, but if you are doing it together try to match your rhythm to hers rather than the other way round.

Change it to a road safety song:
*I can hear Calvin
    walking down the street,
When he sees the red man
    he knows he has to STOP.*
(Hold his feet still until GO)

*I can see Calvin,
    waiting at the kerb,
When he sees the green man
    he knows that he can GO*
(Tap feet until the word STOP).

Many nursery rhymes and songs are well suited to leg walking – try *Jack and Jill, Dr Foster went to Gloucester,* and *See saw sacaradown.*

The grand old Duke of York

1

Oh, the grand old
  Duke of York,
He had ten thousand
  men,
(Walk her legs)

2

He marched them up
  to the top of the hill,
And he marched them
  down again,

3

And when they were
UP they were up,
(Swing her feet right up)

And when they were
DOWN they were
down, (Swing her feet down)

4

And when they were
only half way up,
(Swing from side to side)

5

They were neither UP
(Swing her as high as you can)

6

Nor DOWN
(Drop her down to the floor)

This is Bill Anderson
(Waggle one foot)

This is
  Tom Sim.
(Waggle the other)

Tom called
Bill to fight
And fell over
him. (Cross one foot
  over the other)

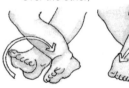

Bill over Tom
And Tom over Bill
(Cross and cross again)

As over and over
(Cross faster)

They rolled
  down
  the HILL
(Drop her between
your knees)

BUMP

Bee baw babbity

Bee baw babbity
  babbity babbity,
Bee baw babbity,
Babbity brewster
  brawly.

Wha learned ye
  to dance, ye to
  dance, ye to dance?
Wha learned ye
  to dance,
Babbity brewster
  brawly?

My mother
  learned me
  to dance . . .

Bend down
  and touch
  your toes . . .

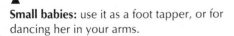

Small babies: use it as a foot tapper, or for dancing her in your arms.

Bigger babies and toddlers: sit her on your knee and walk or dance her legs in rhythm to the song, or simply bounce her. You can play it like *Ring a roses,* tumbling down on the last line of each verse.

Sound-makers for babies to kick

Suspend a balloon at kicking height from a set of Christmas chimes, or a bunch of bells, which are in turn attached very firmly to the ceiling, or above the cot. Let her lie underneath and kick the balloon to make the bells ring. She will still enjoy this game when she is old enough to sit up and bat the balloon with her hands.

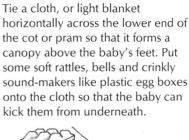

Tie a cloth, or light blanket horizontally across the lower end of the cot or pram so that it forms a canopy above the baby's feet. Put some soft rattles, bells and crinkly sound-makers like plastic egg boxes onto the cloth so that the baby can kick them from underneath.

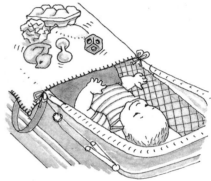

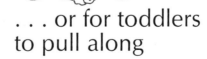

. . . or for toddlers to pull along

String together a large tin can, (*make sure it has no sharp edges*), old metal spoons and saucepan lids, and let your toddler drag them along a suitable place like a concrete path, or your hallway (provided that you and the paintwork can stand it!).

A marvellous leg walker and knee ▶ bouncer combined.

Larger babies and toddlers:

1 This part of the song is a march, so take an ankle in each hand and, with the child on your knee, walk her along.

2 The melody swings into a jig – take a firm hold of her and bounce her on your knee. Try bouncing her particularly high on the word 'away' and on the last 'ho'.

Replace walking with hopping (just raise one foot), jumping (both feet together), swimming with arm movements (why not!).

You can use this song to help hurry along a lagging toddler.

Small babies: hold her in your arms and walk in the first part, then dance around in the second. Exaggerate your movements so that she really feels the change in rhythm.

As soon as she is old enough to have shoulder rides, this is a super song to sing. Again, exaggerate heavy marching steps in the first part, then skip or gallop off with her in the second – best done out of doors.

Rhythm sticks: (see page 37) these can be fun to use instead of actions. Hold them in the baby's hands with her and tap them on the floor for the first part, and against each other for the second.

Rig a jig jig

1

As I was walking
   down the street,
Down the street,
   down the street,
A friend of mine
   I chanced to meet,
Hey ho, hey ho,
   hey ho! And –

2

Rig a jig jig,
   and away we go,
Away we go,
   away we go,
Rig a jig jig,
   and away we go,
Hey ho hey ho,
   hey ho.

Hob shoe hob

Hob shoe hob
Hob shoe hob
Here a nail
   and there a nail,
And that's well shod!

(Tap each foot alternately)

1

Jelly on the plate,
Jelly on the plate,
(Bounce her on your knee)

2

Wibble wobble,
Wibble wobble,
(Wobble her from side to side)
Jelly on the plate.
(Bounce her again)

Biscuits in the tin,
Biscuits in the tin,
(Bounce)
Shake them up,
Shake them up,
(Shake her)
Biscuits in the tin.
(Bounce)

Fire on the floor,
Fire on the floor,
(Bounce)

3

Stamp it out,
Stamp it out,
(Stamp her feet on the floor)
Fire on the floor.
(Bounce)

Candles on the cake,
Candles on the cake,
Blow them out,
Blow them out,
(Bounce)

4

Puff puff puff.
(Blow into her hair or face)

Jack be nimble
Jack be quick
Jack JUMP over
the candlestick

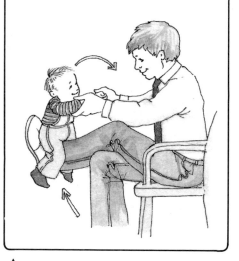

▲
Larger babies and toddlers: cross your legs and sit the baby on your crossed ankle. Hold her hands and gently swing her up and down. Then on 'JUMP', swing your leg up so that she flies up with it and lands with a bump on your knee.

◀This can be a very fast knee bouncer once you have got the rhythm going, but keep it gentle for very small babies who might prefer to lie on their backs and have their legs waved.

A sailor went to sea

A sailor went to sea
  sea sea
To see what he could
  see see see
But all that he could
  see see see

(Bounce her on your knee)

Was the BOTTOM
of the deep blue
sea sea sea.

(Drop her between your knees)

Bouncing ball

See how I'm bouncing,
  bouncing, bouncing,
See how I'm bouncing
  like a ball.

(Bounce her on your knee, or a bed)

You didn't know I
could bounce so high!

You didn't know I
  could sit so still –
See how I'm bouncing,
  bouncing, bouncing,
When I get tired then
  DOWN I fall.

(Drop her between your knees)

◀ Add these verses for a riotous swim or bath:

A sailor went to sea, kick kick . . .

A sailor went to sea, splash splash . . .

A sailor went to sea, bubble bubble . . .
(Blow bubbles in the water with your mouth)

Lie the baby on a bed, take her ankles ▶ and shake her by them (as gently or as vigorously as she is happy with). On 'over' roll her over sideways from her back to her tummy. Confident toddlers can be swung upside down by their ankles and flopped over onto their tummies.

Shake the blanket
Shake the blanket
Turn the blanket
    OVER

**Father and Mother
and Uncle Tom
Got up on the pony
and rode along,**

(Jog her on your knee at walking pace)

Father fell off

(to one side)

And mother fell off,

(to the other side)

**And Uncle Tom rode
on, and on, and on.**

(Bounce faster and faster)

Tinga layo!

1

**Tinga layo! Come,
little donkey, come.
Tinga layo! Come,
little donkey, come.**

2

**Me donkey BUCK
Me donkey LEAP**

3

**Me donkey KICK
wid him two hind feet.**

(Repeat 2 and 3)

4

**Tinga layo! Come,
little donkey, come.
Tinga layo! Come,
little donkey, come.**

▲

A trotting knee rider with a buck, a leap
and a kick in the middle. Bounce small
babies in your arms.

Toddlers: improvise some reins with a belt
or a loop of cord, perhaps with some bells
attached, for the child to hold while you
bounce her. Bigger toddlers will have fun
trotting round the room with you in tow!
You can make a simple hobby horse for
this out of an old sock stuffed with paper
and a broom handle. ▶

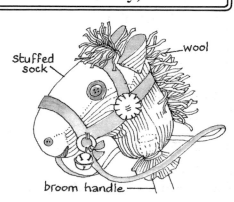

stuffed sock

wool

broom handle

Hop up

Will your horse take us
  walking, Uncle Joe,
  Uncle Joe?
Will your horse take us
  walking, Uncle Joe?
Will your horse take us
  walking, Uncle Joe,
  Uncle Joe?
Don't mind the
  weather so the
  wind don't blow.
Hop up, my ladies,
  three in a row,
Hop up, my ladies,
  three in a row,
Hop up my ladies,
  three in a row,
Don't mind the
  weather so the
  wind don't blow.

Will your horse take us
  trotting . . .
Will you take us for a
  gallop . . .

This is the way the baby rides

This is the way the
  baby rides, trit trot,
  trit trot, trit trot.

(Trot her gently on your knee)

And this is the way the
  jockey rides, a-gallop,
  a-gallop, a-gallop.

(Vigorous bounces)

And this is the way the
  funny clown rides,
  up and over, and
  up and over,
  and DOWN
  to the
  ground
  he goes.

▲
Try making up your own versions, e.g:
This is the way the robot walks, clank clank . . . And this is the way he drinks his oil, glug glug . . . And this is the way he falls apart, crash, bang, scrunch.

Or: *This is the way the rabbit hops . . . And this is the way the kangaroo jumps . . . And this is the way the elephant thumps . . .*

◀ Walk, trot and gallop her on your knee throughout the verse, and in the chorus toss her up in the air on each 'hop up'. Add more verses:
  Will you take us for a JUMP . . .
  Mind you don't take a TUMBLE . . .

Yoghurt pot clip clops

For a very simple instrumental accompaniment, yoghurt pots are easy to hold and clop together. Help a baby by holding them in her hands with her.

Don't expect your toddler to play in rhythm. Just let her have fun joining in while you keep up the rhythm.

Scrubbing song

Scrub your dirty
    hands
Scrub your dirty
    hands
Scrubba dubba
    dub dub
Scrubba dubba
    dub dub
Scrub your dirty
    hands.

▲
Babies and toddlers: a lively song to get the day going or help it towards its close. Change hands to face, knees, tummy, teeth, hair and so on.

Change it to a swimming song:
    Splash your hands around . . .
    Kick out with your feet . . .

And it can help get your toddler involved in the housework:

Scrub this dirty floor . . .

This foot stepped in a puddle of paint,
And this foot trod in the mud!
So down came a thundercloud filled with rain
And splished and sploshed and
    rubbed and scrubbed,
And washed them all clean again.

▲
Tickle her feet as she sits in the bath. Your soapy hand or a sponge is the thundercloud which drops down to wash them.

Make up other verses for her hands, tummy, toes etc.

Pop pop pop

1

Pop pop pop go
    your poppers

2

And zip zip zip go
    your zips

3

With your hat on top

4

and your boots below

5

You can JUMP UP,
    and go, go, go!

Sarah wears her stripey dress

1

Sarah wears her
stripey dress, stripey
dress, stripey dress,
Sarah wears her stripey
dress, all day long.

2

Let's put on your
wellie boots . . .

3

Jamie keep your
hat on . . .

4

Let's put on your
dancing shoes . . .

5

Let's put on our
wriggly fingers . . .

▲
Babies and toddlers: sing about the
clothes she is wearing, run your finger
along stripes, point to spots, flowers,
buttons and bows, and sing about their
colours. Use it for dressing and
undressing.

Toddlers: change the words to include
lots of actions:
Let's put on our stamping shoes . . .
Let's go riding on our bikes . . .
Let's go flying like a bird . . .
Let's go rocking in a boat . . .

Dolly board

Make a dolly board with
poppers to pop, zippers to zip,
and velcro to make that lovely
ripping sound.

Use tough cardboard or
hardboard as a backing and
firmly glue scraps of felt or
cotton, or paint on to it the
basic shape of a dolly. Attach
strips of velcro to the dolly
shape at the waist, neck, cuffs
and ankles. Next cut out clothes
shapes from scraps of material
incorporating poppers and zips,
and sew velcro backing at the
appropriate places.

I went to visit

I went to visit a
    farm one day
I saw a cow
    across the way,
And what do you
    think I heard it say?
MOO MOO MOO!

I went to visit a
    friend one day
I walked in the
    puddles along
    the way,
And what do you think
    I heard them say?
SPLISH SPLASH
    SPLOSH!

I went to see a band
    one day
I heard a drum begin
    to play
And what do you
    think I heard it say?
BOOM BOOM
    BOOM!

Swing song

Up and down, up and down,
Swing me up, and swing
    me down,
Up and down, up and down,
Swing me over street
    and town.
    Push me high I want
        to fly,
    Push me right up to
        the sky,
Up and down, up and down,
Swing me over moon
    and sun . . .

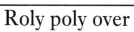

▲
A song to swing to, which is also a lovely lullabye. Other songs for playground swinging are the nursery rhyme *See-saw Marjory Daw* and the *Skye Boat Song* – also both good lullabies.

◀ These are just some of the many ways you can use this song. It can be fun to sing as you are looking at an appropriate picture book (e.g one showing farm animals or a visit to the zoo), or to sing as you go tramping down the street listening out for cats, birds, cars, road diggers, and people at work.

Roly poly over
(Lie her on her front
    and roll her onto her back)

Sit among the clover
(Sit her up)

Take my hand and
    up you stand
(Pull her to her feet)

And AWAY you go.
(Swing her up in the air)

One to make ready
Two to make steady
Three to prepare
And AWAY goes
the mare!

▲
Use this as a race starter or as a walking and swinging rhyme for when there are two of you to swing her up into the air as you walk along.

Riding on a train

We're all riding on a train,
We're all riding on a train,
We're going far away
for the day,
Then we'll all ride
back again.

The guard shuts the
doors on the train –
BANG . . .

(Swing her arm across her chest)

Going very fast
on the train –
clickety clack . . .

(Speed up)

Bouncing up and down
on the train . . .

The driver blows the
whistle on the train –
WOO-WOO . . .

Children clap their
hands on the train –
(clap clap clap) . . .

Coming to the station
on the train . . .

(Slow down)

▲
A sound and action song for both babies and toddlers, which can be changed to riding on a bus, car, aeroplane, horse, your shoulders . . . Change the words and sounds and actions to suit, and fit in your own child's name and her friends' names:
    *We're all riding in a car
    brm brm brm . . .*

*Sally blows the horn on the car
    peep peep peep . . .*
(Press her nose or tummy)

*Alexa works the wipers on the car
    swish swash swish . . .*
(Index fingers move like wipers)

*Leroy is the conductor on the bus
    "Tickets please" . .*

Sound games and toys for babies

Pram, cot and pushchair rattles

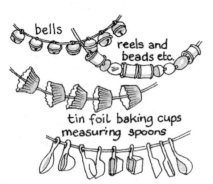

These are easily made and can be changed as soon as she becomes bored with them.

Peekaboo sounds

Play lots of games with bells and rattles with her from birth. Shake them in front of her, then to one side, behind the chair, behind your back. Notice when she first turns towards the sound.

Shakers to make

Small, easily held shakers are best for babies. Fill a plastic herb jar with some rice or cornflakes. Plop a big bead into an empty baby food can and tape another one on top. Here are some more ideas:

Shell rattle: a small transparent plastic box can make a fascinating rattle if you fill it with lovely things for her to look at – sea shells, glass beads, some broken pieces of pottery, dice, etc. Tape it shut very securely.

Bell spray: loop a string of bells, pasta, buttons, or milk bottle tops through two cotton reels taped together to form a handle (or any other suitable tube).

Russian doll rattle: put different-sized containers with lids she can easily remove inside each other, finishing with a prize like a small toy or a biscuit in the smallest container.

Shaker conversations

Rattle one of her shakers, then pass it to her to rattle. Gently take it back and rattle it again. Vary the pattern – rattle it then drop it ('Crash'), rattle it then bang it on a chair, and so on.

Tapping games

Tap together two bricks, spoons, or your hands on a table or chair, and she will copy you as soon as she is able. As in the rattle conversation, try varying the pattern but keep it very simple. (Also converse with her in her own babbling baby talk and add new syllables to the ones she makes.)

Weee-PLOP

A lap game – buy a cardboard tube from a stationers and use it to drop things through into a bucket or large tin can on the floor. Help her to drop small balls, stones, beads, spoons, toys (supervise her so that she doesn't put anything dangerously small in her mouth).

Newspaper scrunch

Give her a pile of old magazines and newspapers, and help her to rip, scrunch and flap them. Imitate the sounds you make with your voice. Make her a trumpet out of a roll of paper and toot through it for her.

Bath sounds and toys

Show her how to blow bubbles through a straw or hosepipe. Drop different-sized containers upside down into the water, and imitate the sounds with your voice. Fill a see-through plastic bottle with a little water, some washing-up liquid and some food dye – as she shakes it, it will fill with coloured bubbles.

Glockenspiel plop

Show her how to drop or run things over the bars of a little glockenspiel (fairly inexpensive ones can be bought, and make a good toy from around three months on). Experiment with different items – a ball, toy car, keys, wooden bricks, feathers, etc.

There are many more sound games to play. Make up your own, and observe how your baby plays with sound herself so that you can help her to extend her experiments as you play together.

Who's that?

Who's that tapping
at the window?
Who's that knocking
at the door?

Thomas tapping
at the window,
Thomas knocking
at the door.

▲

Small babies: hold her in your arms as you sing and tap on a window, door, drum, tabletop, etc.

Bigger babies and toddlers: as soon as she is able, let her do the tapping herself. Take turns with her, but let her play in her own rhythm. Change the words to suit instruments and sounds she can hear, and condense the song if you like:

Who's that ringing on the bells?
Surya ringing on the bells?

Who's that running up the stairs?
Daddy running up the stairs.

Sound games and toys for toddlers

Tap, blow, shake, pluck, scrape

Choose one object with good sound-making potential – an empty, plastic bottle with ridges, a sturdy teapot, a roll of paper – and explore with your toddler every possible way of playing it. You can use a beater (e.g. a chopstick or wooden spoon) to help you. Talk about the sounds you make – whether they are hard, soft, long, short, high or low. Play the game with the shakers, drums, and other instruments you make together.

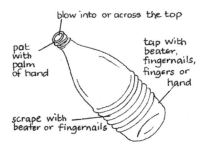

blow into or across the top

pat with palm of hand

tap with beater, fingernails, fingers or hand

scrape with beater or fingernails

Box, tin, bowl

Line up a small cardboard box, a biscuit tin and a plastic bowl (or any other three suitable items) and find yourself and your toddler a beater to tap them. Play a pattern for her to copy, e.g:

box   box   tin   bowl

Change the pattern, but keep it very simple. Invite her to play a pattern for you to copy.

Mouth music

Make up a pattern of mouth sounds – tongue clicks, humming, saying *sh,* yawning, clicking teeth, hissing, saying nonsense syllables – and invite her to copy (this follows on well from baby talk conversations). As above, keep the pattern very simple, perhaps just making one sound, but varying the speed, or the dynamics, pitch or duration. With a bigger toddler, talk about the sounds, whether they are getting slower or faster (speed), louder or softer (dynamics), higher or lower (pitch), longer or shorter (duration),

Roly poly very slowly

Roll your hands round and round each other and let her join in as you repeat each section and change the speed, dynamics, pitch and duration:

Roly poly very slowly (say the words slowly and roll your hands round in slow circles)
Roly poly faster and faster,
Roly poly up, up, up (make your voice and hands go up)
Roly poly down, down down,
Roly poly sh, sh, sh, (whisper and make very small circles)
Roly poly louder and louder (make your voice louder and the circles bigger)
Ro-ly-po-ly ve-ry short (break up the words and make short movements)
Ro–ly–po–ly ve–ry–lo–ng (draw out the words and actions)

Find the money

Collect three or four identical containers. Put some coins into one, and fill the others with beans, making the weight of each container approximately the same. Invite her to find the money by shaking the containers. Let her muddle them up for you to try.

Find the music box

Hide a small music box or toy somewhere in the room, and ask her to try and find it by listening to where the sound is coming from. You may need to help her as this is quite difficult. Then let her hide it for you to find.

Shakers of all shapes and sizes

Make these together, so that your toddler can see and feel the fillings you put in, and help you to decorate the finished instrument.

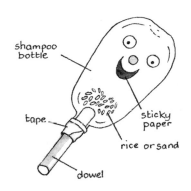

shampoo bottle

tape

sticky paper

rice or sand

dowel

Basic shakers

Any empty, unbreakable container with a secure lid can be used. Fill it with cornflakes, dry breadcrumbs, or milkbottle tops for very soft sounds; rice, lentils or pasta for harder sounds; and coins, beans or metal nuts for *very* loud sounds. With see-through containers, use attractive fillers like shells, beads, dried autumn leaves, or painted pasta. Make your shakers into characters by painting or sticking on faces and attaching wool for hair – let your toddler help you as much as possible.

Macaroni tambourine

Paint some interesting pasta shapes and thread them along with milkbottle tops onto strong wool. String them across a paper or tinfoil plate to make a tambourine.

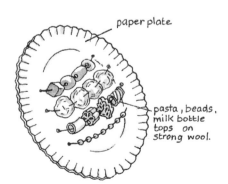

paper plate

pasta, beads, milk bottle tops on strong wool.

Slither box

Put some dry sand into a long flat box, like a chocolate box, seal it all round with tape, and decorate it. Tip it from side to side – the weight and sound of the sand are very satisfying.

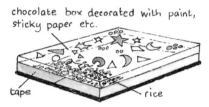

chocolate box decorated with paint, sticky paper etc.

tape   rice

Sand trickler

Join together two or more cylindrical containers (e.g. baby wipes), first cutting holes about 4cm in diameter in the tops and bottoms of each of the inside containers. Pour in a little rice or sand before sealing. Tip it gently and listen to the sand trickling through.

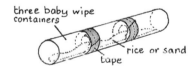

three baby wipe containers

rice or sand

tape

Biscuit tin drum

Decorate a biscuit tin together (or a caterer's size coffee or soup can), then help her to find a variety of beaters to hit it with – a metal spoon, wooden spoon, paint brush, egg whisk, chopstick, etc.

Sound stories

Add sound effects to stories you read or make up together. Many traditional stories lend themselves well to this, e.g. *The Billy Goats Gruff*. Choose an appropriate sound-maker or body sound for each different character and play it whenever they appear. In *The Billy Goats Gruff* you might click together two large buttons for the little billy goat, two yoghurt pots for the middle-size one, and tap a biscuit tin drum for the largest goat.

Make up your own sound stories from events in your toddler's day, 'We walked along the street today – tap tap tap tap (tap knees), and saw the big children on the seesaw – bonk bonk bonk bonk (take her hands in yours and tap them on the table alternately) . . .' Collect new sounds when you go out together.

These are just a few ideas for sound play. Try to introduce them in the course of everyday play, rather than treating them as special events. Make up your own games. Your toddler will be making her own experiments with sound quite naturally, and the games given here are intended to extend and encourage her exploration, and not to be the sole source of it.

Charlie is beating a drum

Charlie is beating a drum
   Boom boom boom
Charlie is beating a drum
   Boom boom boom
Hey there, everyone,
   sit up and listen!
Charlie is beating a drum
   Boom boom boom

Charlie is beating very
   softly...

Simon is clicking his
   tongue...

Annabelle is washing
   her face...

The bees are buzzing
   round the flowers...

The telephone is
   ringing in the hall...

This little goat is
   crossing the bridge...

Richard can you do this?

Richard can you
   do this,
   do this, do this?
Richard can you
   do this
   just like me?

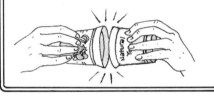

▲
Use this song as you explore sounds – those we can make by playing an instrument in different ways; sounds we can make with our mouths or bodies (clapping, stamping, beating chest, slapping thighs, rubbing palms together); sounds connected with actions like washing, walking, eating; sounds that animals or things like clocks, telephones, or cars make; sounds that occur in stories you read together. It will suit so many different situations.

Also, you can use the song when you are telling your child a story, whether it is a traditional tale or one you have made up about the things she's done during the day, e.g: *'When Valerie jumped out of bed in the morning, she ran down the stairs to see if the postman had brought her anything . . .'*

Valerie is running down the stairs
tap, tap, tap . . .
(Pat knees)

▲
Do any action you like while you sing this song – hand clapping, finger wiggling – and bigger babies and toddlers will join in at their own pace. But it is also particularly useful for exploring instrumental sounds. You might take a homemade shaker each (ones with soft fillings which will not drown your singing), and tap yours gently as you sing, inviting your toddler to copy you. Next time shake it very fast, or jump it across the floor, or tap it with a spoon. Explore different ways of using your voice as you sing – *Richard can you sing high* (stretch up on tiptoe as you sing high); *sing low* (crouch down); *sing softly* (say *sh sh sh* and creep round); *sing loudly* (stamp), and so on. Or try – *Richard can you hisssss* (or hum, yawn, tongue click, etc.). Let her do things for you to copy as well.

Here's a box

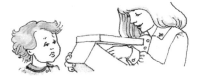

Here's a box
and here's a lid,
I wonder whatever
inside it is hid,
Open the lid and see
what's inside –

Out jumps a tambourine
shake shake shake
Out jumps a tambourine
shake shake shake

Here's a box . . .
Out jumps a jingle bell
ring ring ring
Out jumps a jingle bell
ring ring ring

Here's a box . . .

SNAP

Out jumps a crocodile
snap snap snap
Out jumps a crocodile
snap snap snap

Here's a box . . .
Out jumps a lion
roar roar roar
Out jumps a lion
roar roar roar

Here's a box . . .

Out jumps a spider
tickle tickle tickle
Out jumps a spider
tickle tickle tickle

▲

This can be a sound game or a teaser for toddlers. You can:

Hide some instruments in a box. Play one as you sing the first part (you could pause after 'inside it is hid' to make the sound). Let her guess what it is. Then bring out the instrument and play it as you sing the second part, or give it to her to play.

Pretend you have some animals in the box. Make the sound of one of them as you sing the first part. Can she guess what it is? Then jump up and pretend to be the animal yourself in the second part.

Cup your hands to form a box with the upper hand as the lid. The hand underneath jumps out to be the spider (or mouse) that runs all over the toddler tickling her.

Find a large cardboard box for your toddler to hide in and jump out of as a lion, elephant, witch, or robot.

Aiken Drum

There was a man lived in the moon,
   lived in the moon, lived in the moon,
There was a man lived in the moon,
   and his name was Aiken Drum.

And he played upon a ladle, a ladle,
   a ladle,
He played upon a ladle, and his
   name was Aiken Drum.

And he played upon a tea cup,
   a tea cup, a tea cup,
He played upon a tea cup and his
   name was Aiken Drum.

And he played upon a saucepan lid . . .

▲
This is a fine dancing song for small babies, while larger babies and toddlers will enjoy the huge variety of sounds they can make. Sing it when you are working in the kitchen, where there are plenty of 'instruments' to hand, or round the house. Use it as a treasure hunt for bigger toddlers, sending them off to search for things which Aiken Drum can play on.

You can string up some of these on a long line between chairs – suspended they will sound better, and louder!

Sandpaper blocks

Glue or pin sandpaper to small blocks of wood, then rub them together to make the sound of a steam engine.

Coffee coffee

Coffee coffee,
   coffee coffee,
Egg and chips,
   egg and chips,
Cheese and biscuits,
   cheese and biscuits,
Jelly and cream,
   jelly and cream,
Sooooooooooooooup!

▲
A song that mimics the sounds of the old steam engines.

Small babies: push and pull her legs like pistons as she lies on her back.

Larger babies and toddlers: take her hands as she sits on your knee and move her arms like pistons, getting faster and faster until on 'sooooup' you pretend to pull the train's whistle. Reverse the order of the words and slow down again.

Small babies: walk with her in ▶ your arms so that she feels the rhythm. If she's confident and firm enough you can swing her from side to side like the pendulum in the clock.

The last line can indicate an action e.g.:
It's time to tap your nose,

Tap tap tap tap
Tap tap tap tap
Tap tap tap tap
It's time to tap your nose.

Or, as she lies back in a bouncing cradle or is propped up on cushions you can sing the song and tap a pair of rhythm sticks.

Bigger babies and toddlers: use it as an action song as above but with more elaborate actions. It can be a going-to-bed song:
It's time to brush your teeth . . .
It's time to wash your face . . .
It's time to kiss goodnight . . .

Help her to hold a pair of rhythm sticks and tap them together. Bigger toddlers can do this for themselves. Don't be concerned about erratic rhythm and certainly don't try to correct it – she is still gaining confidence in hitting the sticks together. Just click your own sticks with a steady *tick tock* beat, and in time she will do the same.

Change the last line to:
It's time to tap very softly/ loudly/quickly/slowly . . .

Insert other sounds:
The bell goes ding-a-ling . . .
The drum goes boom boom . . .
The car goes brm brm . . .

Tick tock

The clock says tick tock
The clock says tick tock
The clock says tick tock
It's time to say hello.

Hello teddy, hello dolly, hello lion,
It's time to say hello.

The clock says tick tock . . .
It's time to stamp your feet.
Stamp, stamp, stamp . . .

Chop chop chop chop
Cut off the bottom and cut off the top
All the rest goes into the pot
Chop chop chop chop.

▲
Lay one rhythm stick on the floor – the carrot – while you chop it with the other – the knife.

Rhythm sticks

Cut two lengths of dowel, about 2.5cm in diameter and 18cm long (an old broom handle is good), and you have a pair of rhythm sticks all ready to click together.

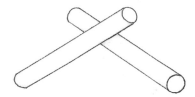

Use them to accompany *Hickory dickory dock.*

Kangaroos like to hop

1

Kangaroos like to hop –
HOP HOP HOP HOP

2

Horses like to trot –
CLIP CLOP CLIP
CLOP CLIP CLOP

3

And frogs like to leap –
WEEEEEEEEEE

4

But I like to fall in a
heap – BONK!

▲

Babies and toddlers big and small love this one – it is a wonderful song for cheering them up and getting a move on when their feet are dragging. Bigger toddlers can do the actions themselves.

Make up your own verses and actions.
Here's another to try:
  Now a rocket goes up – WHOOSH
  (Toss her high up in the air)

And a diver comes down – SPLOOSH
(Drop her down again)
A pendulum likes to swing – TICK TOCK TICK TOCK
(Swing her from side to side)
But I am a bird on the wing – WEEEE
(Swing her right round you in a big circle)

Come along, John

Come along, John,
  hush your talking,
Take my hand and
  we'll go a-walking,
Walk along, John,
  with your green
  shoes on,
Walk along, John,
  with your green
  shoes on.

Come along, Carla,
  hush your talking,
Take my hand, and
  we'll go a-jumping
Jump along, Carla,
  with your blue
  hat on . . .

Come along, Rachel,
  hush your talking,
Take my hand, and
  we'll get a-working,
Come along,
  Rachel, let's wash
  your socks . . .

Golden corn

Golden corn is growing so high,

The wind blows east

And the wind blows west

And the little brown mouse runs down to her nest.

◄ Make up your own actions to suit the occasion. It can be a walking down the street song, a going to bed song, or a useful distraction for a small, upset or tired toddler, e.g:

Come along, Jamie,
hush your crying,
Mummy's got a cuddle (game/treat)
to get you smiling,
Come along, Jamie, let's
play with the bricks,
Come along, Jamie, let's
play with the bricks.

(If this suggestion doesn't work, go on adding others until you find one that does!)

Hold her hands and jump her up and ► down on each word, then swing her into your arms on 'three'. Turn her upside down so she can pretend to catch fishes.

American jump
American jump
One two three.

Under the sea
Catching fishes
Catching fishes
for tea!

▲
Babies: hold her in your arms and crouch down low, then lift her high in the air, sway her from side to side, then bring her down into your arms and run your fingers down to her toes.

The actions rise and fall with the melody line. Here is another verse to sing to this melody, to which you can add more rising and falling actions:

Here comes the window cleaner
climbing up the ladder.
He cleans the windows to make
them shine,
Then he runs down the ladder
and he says 'That's fine!'.

As you climb stairs together sing a rising scale, and as you come down, sing down the scale again. Sing a rising scale as you make a tower of bricks, and let your voice slide down from a high note, as together you watch a raindrop slipping down the window pane.

Early in the morning

1

Early in the morning
at eight o'clock,

(Walk her legs)

2

You can hear the
postman's knock

(Tap the floor, or a table)

3

JUMP UP Josie,

4

Open up the door,

(Swing arm open)

5

One letter,

two letters,

three letters,

four.

CLAP
CLAP
CLAP
CLAP

Dabbling ducks

1

All the little ducks
turn upside down,
Upside down,
upside down,
All the little ducks
turn upside down,
When they dabble
at the bottom
of the pond.

2

All the little tails go
wiggle waggle
wiggle . . .

3

snap

All the little beaks go
snap, snap, snap . . .

▲
In verses 1 and 2, babies and small
toddlers can be turned upside down and
waggled bodily in your arms. Bigger
toddlers can try the hand actions.

Open, shut them

Open, shut them,
(Hands)
Open, shut them,
Give a little clap,
(Clap)
Open, shut them,
Open, shut them,
Lay them on your lap.

Open, shut them,
(Fingers)
Open, shut them,
Give them all a shake,
(Shake)
Open, shut them,
Open, shut them,
Keep them all awake.
(Shake)

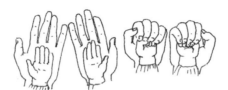

Open, shut them,
(Arms)
Open, shut them,
Don't get in a muddle.
Open, shut them,
Open, shut them,
Give yourself a cuddle.

The elephant goes like
this, like that,
(Thump floor, or table and sway
from side to side)

He's terribly
big,

and he's terribly fat.

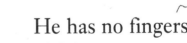

He has no fingers
(Wiggle them)

He has no toes
(Tickle them)

But goodness, gracious,
what a nose!

Tommy Thumb

Tommy Thumb,
Tommy Thumb,
Where are you?
(Hide thumb)

Here I am,
Here I am,
(Produce it)

How do you do?
(Bend it three times)

Peter Pointer

Toby Tall

Ruby Ring

Baby Small

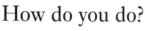

Small babies: cover her hand in yours, stroke or tap each finger, then waggle it.

Bigger babies and toddlers: sing it with the actions given above. Make a sticky paper face for each finger if you like. Change it to make new games:

Mr Foot: change Tommy Thumb to Mr Foot, Tummy Button, Knobbly Knee, etc. With small babies pat or tickle each part.

Dance, Thumbkin, dance

1

Dance, Thumbkin, dance,
Dance, Thumbkin, dance,
Thumbkin cannot dance alone
(Waggle thumb)

Dance, Pointer, dance . . .

Dance, Tallman, dance . . .

2

So dance you merry men every one,
Dance, Thumbkin, dance.
(All fingers dance)

Dance, Ringman, dance . . .

Dance, Baby, dance . . .

▲

Bathtime and swimming: use it to encourage a reluctant child to wash, or splash hands and feet in the pool – change the last line to 'splish splash splosh'.

Peekaboo: hide a bell, finger puppet, or Peter Pointer behind your back, then produce it. Last line – 'Peek-a- BOO!'

Jack-in-the-box: a toddler can hide in a cardboard box (sing her name), then jump out at 'Here I am', and shake hands with you.

Dressing: sing it while looking for a head stuck down inside a jumper, or hands and feet lost in sleeves and trousers.

▲

You can make a little paper crown for your fingers or hers to wear in turn, or slip a ring over the dancing finger – just to add to the fun of distinguishing between them.

Small babies: hold her in your arms and in the first part waggle your thumb, then dance with her as you sing:
Thumbkin cannot dance alone,
So dance little baby, dance
with him,
Dance, baby, dance,
Dance, baby, dance.

Peter and Paul

**Two little dickie birds
Sitting on a wall,**

(Hold up both index fingers)

**One named
Paul,**

Peter,

(Waggle one finger)

**The other
named Paul.**

(Waggle the other)

**Fly away,
Peter,**

(Fly the first away
behind your back)

**Fly away,
Paul,**

(Fly away the second)

**Come back,
Peter**

(Bring back the first)

**Come back,
Paul.**

(Bring back the second)

Finger and hand puppets

A baby will find fingerplays more interesting if you have some finger puppets to waggle while you sing. As she gets older, she will start waggling her own fingers and will gradually get better at waggling them individually. Some of the simplest things can often be the most effective. Here are some ideas for instant finger puppets:

1 Using a felt-tip pen, draw little faces on the tips of your fingers.

2 Put sticky paper faces on your fingertips or on the fingers of a glove. You can cut the fingers off an old one if you like.

3 Cut out a strip of paper about 4cm deep. Fasten it in a circle big enough to fit over your thumb. Staple together the top edge and cut slits in it to make hair. Draw on a face.

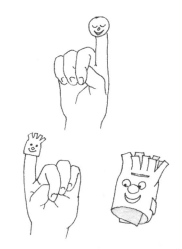

4 Two little dickie birds:

Glove puppets can also be easy to make and can enliven songs. Sew together two outgrown socks to make a variety of characters, e.g:

Make a Jack-in-the-box puppet and use it when you sing *Peek-a-boo, Jack-in-the-box* or *Here's a box*. The puppet can play mystery sounds inside the box (rattle, bell, keys, tambourine). Ask a bigger toddler to guess what they are.

By'm bye

By'm bye
By'm bye
Stars
  shining,
Number, number one,
  number two,
  number three,
  number four.
Good Lord, by'm bye,
  by'm bye, Good
  Lord, by'm bye.

(Rock her on your knee)

By'm bye
By'm bye
  Finger
  counting . . .

(Touch or stroke each finger in turn)

Buttons
  shining . . .

(Point to them)

Toes
  twinkling . . .

Poppers
  popping . . .

Old Davey Jones

1

Old Davey Jones had
  one little sailor,
Old Davey Jones had
  one little sailor,
Old Davey Jones had
  one little sailor,
One little sailor girl.

(Hold up little finger and dance it)

2

He had one, he had two,
  he had three little
  sailors,
Four, he had five,
  he had six little sailors,
Seven, he had eight, he
  had nine little sailors,
Ten little sailor girls.

(Draw out each finger in turn)

3

Old Davey Jones had
  ten little sailors . . .

(Wiggle all fingers)

4

He had ten,
  he had nine . . .

(Fold down each finger in turn)

◀ This rocking song can be used as a lullabye and for all kinds of counting. When you have a group of small children together you can count all the feet, hands, heads, noses, etc.

▲
Change the words to include your child's name; change girl to boy. Use it to count items such as buttons, pebbles, toys:
Little Charlie Roberts had
* one little pebble . . .*

Lollipops

Five sticky lollipops
fixed on sticks,

(Waggle five fingers)

Take a sticky lollipop
and lick lick lick.

(Hold up one and lick it)

Four sticky
lollipops . . .

Three sticky
lollipops . . .

Two sticky
lollipops . . .

One sticky lollipop . . .

No sticky lollipops
fixed on sticks.
No sticky lollipops
to lick lick lick.

(Hold up fist)

1

Here are the candles
red, white and blue,
To put on a birthday
cake for you.

Now take a
deep breath
and get
ready to blow – 2

3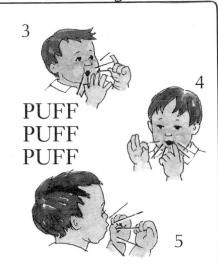

PUFF
PUFF
PUFF

4

5

Out they go!

Five little peas in a peapod pressed, 1

First one grew 2

then another, 3

then all the rest. 4

They got bigger,
and bigger,
and BIGGER,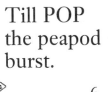

Till POP
the peapod
burst.

5

6
CLAP

45

Rockaway

Rockaway my little,
   rock little baby,
Rockaway my precious
   beautiful baby,
Lalee, rockaway.

Wherever you may be,
   there will be your joy,
Those who love you
   darling,
   see the heaven of God.
Lalee, rockaway.

Wise little charmer,
   many heart stealer,
Wise lessons you
   teach through
   your happy play.
Lalee, rockaway.

Strong little baby,
   wonderful baby,
Proud you make
   everyone as we rock
   your cradle.
Lalee, rockaway.

1

Wherever love is,
   there you will
   ever live,
Ever living you fill
   our hearts with
   sweet love.
Lalee, rockaway.

Mobiles

1 Cut out three or four cardboard teddies (copy the shape illustrated here), decorate them, and tie small bells, or bunches of milk-bottle tops to their hands and feet. String them one below the other (ear to toe) on elastic. Attach a big bead or cotton reel on a string to the last teddy's toe so that the baby can pull it and make all the teddies bounce and jingle.

2 Dangle strings of milkbottle tops, beads, bells and coloured paper streamers from a wire coat-hanger, and hang it above the baby's reach.

3 Cut out a crescent moon and stars from a tinfoil plate. Dangle them on threads from a chopstick or coat-hanger

2

3

All the pretty horses

Hush-a-bye, don't
  you cry,
Go to sleepy,
  little baby.
When you wake, you
  shall have a cake
And all the pretty
  little horses.

Black and bay,
  dapple and grey
Coach and six
  white horses.

Up the wooden hill

You're a sleepy baby, I am tired too,
Close your eyes for Mam and I'll tell you
    what we'll do.
We'll tiptoe very quietly, so nobody can hear,
And we'll go up the wooden hill to Bedfordshire.

You're fragrant as a flower and your smile is like
    the sun,
Close your eyes for Mam for her work it isn't done.
Nothing's going to harm you, you can sleep
    without a care,
When you go up the wooden hill to Bedfordshire.

I've rocked you on my shoulder, I've walked and
    walked the floor,
Close your eyes for Mammy and I will not ask
    for more.
All the songs I ever knew I've sung them
    in your ear,
Now *please* go up the wooden hill to Bedfordshire.

Your Mammy and your Dad need some loving
    of their own,
Close your eyes for Mammy: you'll not be
    all alone.
For when you are asleep there'll be a creaking
    on the stair,
And we'll come up the wooden hill to
    Bedfordshire.

Acknowledgements

The publishers would like to thank the following for permission to reproduce their copyright material:

Leonora Davies for *I can hear Daniel*
David Evans for *Can you play at peekaboo?*
Sandra Kerr for *Roly poly over* and *Up the wooden hill*
Surya Kumari for *Rockaway* and *Tārangam*
Leon Rosselson for *One two three*
Mavis de Mierre for *Tick tock*
Harriet Powell for *Riding on a train*
Cynthia Raza for *Spots spots spots*
Schroder Music Co. for *Everybody says sit down* by Malvina Reynolds, © Schroder Music Co. (ASCAP) 1961. Used by permission. All rights reserved.
Margaret Shephard for *Dabbling ducks* and *Golden Corn*
Tamar Swade for the verse words and melody of *Here's a box* and the melody of *Where oh where?*
Tro-Essex Music Ltd for *Hop up, my ladies* adapted and arranged by John A. Lomax and Alan Lomax, © 1957 Tro-Essex Music Ltd, Suite 207, Plaza 535, Kings Road, London SW10 0SZ. International copyright secured. All rights reserved. Used by permission.
Westminster Music Ltd for *Kangaroos like to hop* by Leon Rosselson, © 1968 Westminster Music Ltd, Suite 207, Plaza 535 Kings Road, London SW10 0SZ. International copyright secured. All rights reserved. Used by permission.

The following are by the author, Sheena Roberts: *Where oh where?* (words), *Clap clap clap* (words), *Ticklebird* (words), *What shall we do with a lazy Katie?* (words), *Macaroni girl* (words), *Pop pop pop*, *Swing song* (words), *Charlie is beating her drum* (words), *Coffee coffee* (melody), *Lollipops* (words), *This foot stepped in a puddle of paint*, *Chop chop*, *Here are the candles*.

All suggestions for extra verses are by Sheena Roberts.

Every effort has been made to trace and acknowledge copyright owners. If any right has been omitted, the publishers offer their apologies, and will rectify this in subsequent editions following notification.

First published in 1987 by Macdonald & Co (Publishers) Ltd

This edition published in 1991 by Playsongs Publications
Reprinted 1993, 1995, 1997 (with new cover), 1999, 2001, 2004 (twice), 2006

© text Sheena Roberts 1987
© illustrations and sound recording Sheena Roberts 1991
© cover illustration by Jo Kelly 1997
Cover design by Jo Kelly and Simon Ray–Hills

Printed in Great Britain by St Edmundsbury Press Ltd, Bury St Edmunds, Suffolk
Book and cassette ISBN 0-9517112-0-2
Book and CD ISBN 0-9517112-1-0

For a catalogue of all our titles please contact
Playsongs Publications Ltd, Wimbish Lower Green, Saffron Walden, Essex CB10 2XH

www.playsongs.co.uk